Before the Next Step

Step

"Questions Before I Do"

Carrington & Ashley Brown

DEDICATION

To my mother Annette who always
promoted sharing the truth, not just the facts.

–Ashley Brown

To all the failed relationships of my parents
that provided me the perfect blueprint of
what not to do in a relationship.

-Carrington Brown

CONTENTS

Acknowledgments

Introduction

ACKNOWLEDGMENTS

God. Thank you for your wisdom and direction that never ceases to amaze us. Thank you for entrusting us with this assignment.

INTRODUCTION

When you know, you know right? Well, maybe. In the beginning of a relationship it is easy to think you know your partner well. Many people dive into relationships, ready to take the next step without truly knowing the character or beliefs of their mate. If you are seriously dating someone, there are questions that should be asked and conversations that should be had before marriage. Sometimes the excitement of what the future may hold causes important topics to be left unvisited. Sadly, many couples rush towards marriage as soon as they experience the initial burst of romance and prematurely enter relationships bypassing red flags and missing opportunities to get to know one another on a deeper level.

Committing your heart to someone is a huge decision. If you choose poorly, you could suffer years of heartache. This heartache could lead to depression, sickness, divorce or much worse. However, if you choose wisely, you could enjoy a lifetime of intimate love, passion and purpose. Dating is a prelude to marriage, and marriage is one of the first declarations given by God to mankind. It is a sacred covenant that you want to treat with the upmost care.

The good news is that as a Christian, you are not alone in your decision-making process. You have Jesus Christ within you and he freely offers His divine wisdom in every situation. Therefore, you don't have to rely on your emotions or limited understanding. God wants the best for you! He gave you the mind of Christ so you can see life from His perspective. When you do so, you save yourself from unnecessary drama and heartache. God gives you discernment which directs you towards healthy relationships and dissuades you from negative ones.

In order to have a fruitful relationship, one of the prerequisites is to create a space where individuals have the freedom to communicate openly and honestly, free of judgement. This book is a tool for improving relationships and getting to know your potential spouse on a deeper level *before taking the next step.* It is designed to challenge you, grow you and excite you about the next chapter of your life. It poses over 300 questions that invite you to explore the depths of one another, while navigating through deep and thought provoking scenarios.

We encourage you to push beyond the simple yes or no, and open up the windows of transparency. These questions are meant to guide intellectually stimulating conversations, not interrogation. So be vulnerable, reveal flaws, show your heart, and allow this book to take you to a new level of intimacy. The next step is waiting for you. Welcome!

1

TABLE TALK

(Personal Questions)

"We all suffer from the preoccupation that there exists…in the loved one, perfection."

- Sidney Poitier

1. Do you love who you are?

2. What do you respect most about yourself?

3. What are your dreams and aspirations?

4. Who or what inspires you?

5. Are you throwing your full self at life?

6. How ambitious would you consider yourself to be?

7. Do you believe the direction of your life is determined by your thoughts?

8. What are your long term goals and are you on track to achieve them?

9. What is your 5-10 year plan?

10. Are you satisfied with your current level of achievement in life?

11. Is there anything preventing you from having the lifestyle you dream of?

12. Which is worse failing or never trying?

13. When it's all said and done, will you have said more than you have done?

14. Are you efficient at getting things done, or do you struggle with procrastination?

15. What do you like most about your job?

16. What would you change about your job?

17. If you won a million

dollars, would you quit your

job?

18. What are you most

grateful for?

19. What are your

weaknesses and how are you

working on them?

20. If my dreams and goals

sounded unrealistic would you

still support me or encourage

me to pursue a different path?

21. How can your significant

other help you accomplish your

goals?

22. Have you read any books

that altered your perception of

yourself or the world?

23. What is the title of the

last book you completed?

24. Have you watched any documentaries that impacted your life in a meaningful way? If so, what were they and what were the lessons learned?

25. Since we have limited time on this earth, why do we do so many things we don't like and like so many things we don't do?

26. When was a time in your life that you were most proud of yourself?

27. When someone asks you for your opinion on a topic do you give your honest opinion?

28. Is there something that you've dreamt of doing for a long time that you have yet to do? If so, why haven't you accomplished it?

29. Are you doing work that you believe in, or are you settling for what you are doing?

30. Have you ever lived on your own?

31. How long have you been responsible for providing for yourself?

32. What are your hobbies?

33. What do you do for fun?

34. What would constitute a perfect day for you?

35. Are you an introvert or an extrovert?

36. Do you like pets?

37. Do you consider pets members of your family?

38. Would you be willing to take care of my pet if I were on vacation?

39. Do you have a fear of

flying?

40. Are you open to traveling

internationally?

41. Have you ever lived

abroad?

42. What is one thing you

would like to change about the

world?

43. How do you feel about cursing?

44. How do you feel about your significant other cursing?

45. How do you feel about me farting or burping around you?

46. Do you drink alcohol? If so how often?

47. Do you keep alcohol in your home?

48. How do you feel about your significant other drinking alcohol?

49. Do you smoke?

50. Would you marry a smoker?

51. Have you in the past or do you currently do recreational drugs?

52. Do you have any addictions?

53. Do you gamble?

54. Would you like to be famous?

55. Do you play video games? If so, how much time

does it consume in your daily

life?

56. Do you have any

prejudices?

57. Do you find yourself pre-

judging people based on their

appearance or material

possessions?

58. Have you committed a

crime or been to prison?

59. Have you ever committed a murder?

60. Would you consider someone who has committed a murder or an egregious offense as a possible spouse?

61. Do you check your cellphone first thing in the morning?

62. Do you think it's appropriate to have your cellphone out during a date or while spending quality time?

63. Are you willing to give up time on your job to spend more time with your family?

64. How do you feel about your significant other having tattoos or piercings?

65. Do you snore?

66. Do you have any insecurities? If so what are they?

67. What makes you happy?

68. What do you fear?

69. When was the last time you cried in front of someone else? By yourself?

70. Are there any television broadcasts that you avoid watching? If so what are they and why?

71. Does your personality change when you are hungry?

72. How do you act when you are tired?

73. What irritates you?

74. How do you handle conflict?

75. What is your opinion about lazy people?

76. Do you vote?

77. What political issues are important to you?

78. Do you believe that two people with different political views can have a successful

marriage?

79. In what ways do you give

back to the community?

80. How important is it that

you contribute time and money

to charity?

81. Do you take advantage of

opportunities to help someone

in need?

82. If you could offer a child in a situation similar to what you grew up in one piece of advice, what would it be?

83. How important is celebrating birthdays and holidays to you?

84. How important is it to receive gifts on holidays and birthdays?

2

EAT CLEAN TRAIN DIRTY

(Questions on Health and Fitness)

"Take care of your body. It's the only place you have to live."

-Jim Rohn

85. Do you even lift bro?

86. Do you view your body as a temple?

87. How important is a healthy lifestyle and exercising?

88. What does your diet consist of?

89. How often do you eat outside of your home?

90. How would you describe

your current state of health?

91. What are the details of

your medical history? Are you

currently having any health

issues?

92. Are you currently taking

any medications?

93. Have you ever been treated for any mental disorders?

94. Do you believe that taking care of your physical and mental health is a part of honoring your marriage vows?

95. How do you take care of your emotional health?

96. Do you have any

allergies?

97. Do you have any genetic

diseases in your family or a

history of cancer, heart disease,

or chronic illness?

98. Does your family have a

history of mental or physical

illness?

99. Do you carry the sickle cell trait?

100. Are you willing to take a HIV test?

101. Have you ever had a sexually transmitted disease?

102. Do you have health insurance?

103. Is weight control important to you?

104. Is your significant

others weight control important

to you?

105. If I were to gain or

lose a significant amount of

weight, how would you

approach me about it?

106. Are you a member of

a gym? If so how much time do

you spend there every week?

107. What is your opinion on my approach to health?

3

WEALTH AND POVERTY

(Questions on Finances)

"I had plastic surgery last week. I cut up my credit cards."

–Henny Youngman

108. What is your current financial situation?

109. Do you keep a personal budget?

110. How well are you at managing your money?

111. Would you say you currently live above or below your means?

112.
Do you have a

savings account?

113.
How do you feel

about having separate bank

accounts?

114.
Do you pay your bills

on time?

115.
What are your total

debts?

116. Are you paying off your debts?

117. Do you understand the concept of debt stacking?

118. How many credit cards do you have?

119. What is the current condition of your credit?

120. Where does the majority of your money go to?

121. Do you pay alimony

or child support?

122. Are you willing to

downsize temporarily in order

for us to be in a position of

financial freedom in the future?

123. What income bracket

do you see yourself in, in the

next 10 years?

124. How will we build

our financial portfolio?

125. How do you feel

about loaning people money?

126. How often do you

lend people money?

127. Would you loan

money without consulting your

significant other first?

128. Do you financially support any of your family (Parents, cousins, aunts…etc.)?

129. Have you now or in the past been responsible or supportive of others financially? If so, for whom? Are you still currently?

130. If we were in a position where we were on a tight budget, would you still be willing to give back and help

those in need monetarily?

131. Are you

uncomfortable discussing

finances within our

relationship?

132. What are your views

on how money should be

managed in marriage?

133.
If we get married, which expenses are obligated to who?

134.
Who do you think should be in charge of our finances?

135.
Are you comfortable with your significant other making more money than you?

136. If I was the main financial provider and I did not want that role anymore, would you be willing to accept that responsibility?

137. If we were to hit a financial crisis what would our back up plan be?

138. Do you understand the importance of the proper life insurance as a family?

139. Do you feel like it is important to save for retirement?

140. How are you currently saving for retirement?

4

FINDING FAITH

(Questions on Spirituality)

"God is limitless in His love, and asks that we at least make the effort to be limitless in ours."

-Marianne Williamson

141. Have you accepted

Christ as your personal savior?

142. How do you feel

about religious people?

143. Are you comfortable

talking about God?

144. Did you grow up in

church?

145. Do you currently belong to a church? If so, what is the denomination?

146. What are your views on denominations?

147. Would you consider yourself a God fearing man or woman?

148. Have you ever been turned off or uninterested in religion?

149. Do you believe there is a difference between having a relationship with God and being religious?

150. What are your beliefs about salvation and Jesus?

151. Is it important for us to have the same spiritual beliefs?

152. Do you believe baptism is necessary to go to Heaven?

153. Have you been baptized?

154. How do you view God in regards to his nature?

155. Describe what your personal relationship with God looks like?

156. If today was judgement day could God say he knows you?

157. Does your lifestyle reflect your beliefs in God? If so, how?

158. Do you believe you are walking in God's purpose for your life?

159. What role does prayer play in your life?

160. How often do you pray?

161. Do you feel comfortable praying in front of people?

162. Is praying as a couple

important to you?

163. How often do you

read the bible?

164. When was a time

where your faith was tested?

165. Do you seek God first

in all things?

166. How often do you

attend church?

167. What ministries are you currently involved in?

168. Are you aware of what your calling is in ministry?

169. How do you represent God outside of the church building?

170. Are you comfortable expressing your beliefs?

171. Have you had any supernatural experiences with God?

172. Do you have any spiritual mentors?

173. Have you sought God's purpose regarding our relationship?

174. How can we reflect God's love in our relationship?

175. How will we

determine which church to

attend?

176. Have you had any

supernatural experiences?

177. Are you afraid of

death?

178. What does it mean to

you when the bible says

"Husbands, love your wives,

just as Christ loved the church

and gave himself up for her?"

179. If you completed the

task God asked of you and no

one took notice, would you be

satisfied or would your heart

long for the worlds approval?

5

GOOD COMPANY

(Questions on Family and Friends)

"If you judge people, you have no time to love them"

-Mother Teresa

180. What does loyalty

mean to you?

181. Would you break the

law to save a loved one?

182. How important is

family to you?

183. How many siblings

do you have?

184. How is your

relationship with your father?

185. How is your

relationship with your mother?

186. What is your

relationship like with your

family?

187. Are your parents still

married?

188. Were you brought up

in a single parent home?

189. How close is your

family?

190. How often do you all

get together?

191. How is the

environment at family get-

togethers?

192. What is the culture of your family?

193. What are your favorite childhood memories?

194. What does friendship mean to you?

195. Who is your best friend?

196. How do you feel

about me having friends of the

opposite sex?

197. Is it okay to go out to

lunch with a co-worker of the

opposite sex?

198. What characteristics

would your friends use to

describe you?

199. Does your beliefs match the beliefs of those of your inner circle?

200. Are there any cultural differences within your family that I need to be made aware of?

201. Have you ever been in a position where you had to forgive a family member for multiple offenses to keep the peace in your family?

202. Do you currently harbor unforgiveness towards any of your family members? If so, what is keeping you from forgiving them and moving on?

203. Do you find yourself repeating the same lifestyle patterns of your relatives?

204. Is there anything in your family history that makes you feel ashamed or self-conscious?

205. When is an appropriate time to introduce each other to our families?

206. How does your family and friends feel about our relationship?

207. How much influence does your family and friends have on our relationship?

208. How would you

handle a situation if a member

of your family was disrespectful

towards me?

209. If I had an issue with

one of your friends, could I tell

you about it?

210. How did your parents

discipline you?

211. If you could change anything about the way you were raised, what would it be?

212. What morals and beliefs did your family instill in you?

213. How does your family background influence your beliefs?

214. If we get married, how involved do you think the in-laws should be?

215. Are you open to allowing a family member to live with us? (Long term or short term?

6

FORGIVE TO FLOURISH

(Questions on Dealing with the Past)

"I have no friends, I have no enemies only teachers."

-Unknown

216.
Is there anything from your past that I should be aware of?

217.
Which past decisions affected your future the most?

218.
Are you still in love with anyone from your past?

219.
Do you still converse with anyone from your past relationships?

220. Are you healed from your past relationships?

221. Have you broken all soul ties from previous relationships?

222. Do you keep pictures or memorabilia from past relationships? Why or why not?

223. Have you ever lived with a previous partner? Why

did you choose to live together before marrying? What did this experience teach you?

224. Have you had issues with infidelity?

225. Have you ever been dishonest in past relationships? If so how?

226. Do you have trust issues?

227. Have you ever been in an abusive relationship?

228. What is your opinion on domestic violence within relationships?

229. Have you ever been engaged or married?

230. Have you been a victim of sexual injustice?

231. How has your past relationships affected your views on relationships & dating?

232. Is there anything that I have done to hurt you in the past that you are still holding on to?

233. Are there any issues that we need to address before taking the next step?

THE PERFECT MATCH

(Questions on Relationships)

"Being someone's first love may be great, but to be their last is beyond perfect."

-Unknown

77

234. What is your love language? (Gifts, quality time, words of affirmation, acts of service, and physical touch (intimacy))

235. What is your view on monogamous relationships?

236. At what age do you desire to be married?

237. What are your reasons

for wanting to be married?

238. Would you marry

outside of your religion?

239. Are you open to pre-

marital counseling?

240. Do you believe in

prenuptial agreements? If no,

why not?

241. What do you believe your role is as a wife or husband?

242. What are your expectations in marriage?

243. What is your biggest fear in marriage?

244. Do you think that having a child out of wedlock is reason for getting married?

245. What does it mean to

submit as a wife?

246. What does it look like

to lead as a husband?

247. Would you consider

me your best friend?

248. Do you trust me?

249. Do you feel

comfortable being emotionally

vulnerable around me?

250. Do you believe that past relationships should be left in the past and not talked about in our current relationship?

251. What are your views on divorce? Is it optional?

252. What are some reasons you would be willing to get a divorce?

253. What are your deal

breakers in a relationship?

254. What is your

communication style? Do you

prefer direct and to the point

communication or a soft

approach?

255. What does it look like

to communicate clearly and

effectively?

256. How should I handle the days when you are in a foul mood?

257. When you get irritated do you like to talk immediately or do you need time to yourself before a discussion?

258. Do you have an issue with compromising?

259. What is the one thing you love most about our relationship?

260. What do you consider a date night and how often would you like to have them?

261. Do you feel it is necessary to inform one another prior to inviting over house guest?

262. How do you feel about your significant other going on vacations without you?

263. Are you okay with me being a stay at home mom?

264. Are you okay with me being a stay at home dad?

265. What is your ideal budget for a wedding?

266. How many guests would you like at your wedding?

267. Where would you like to have a honeymoon?

268. How often would you like to have family vacations?

269. Are you against having a television in the bedroom?

270. If I began to slack in my hygiene are you comfortable enough to let me know?

271. Do I have any habits or tendencies that concern you?

272. Is innocent flirting appropriate?

273. Are you willing to relocate?

274. If you had to move outside of your current state or country, where would you relocate to and why?

275. Are you comfortable with my level of ambition?

276. How do you feel about having guns in the home?

277. What is your

preference on where we spend

holidays?

278. Do you have any

family traditions that you would

like to maintain for the

holidays?

279. How important is it

that you always look your best?

280. How important is your significant other's appearance?

281. How important is it who pays for dinner?

282. Can you cook? What are your expectations when it comes to who cooks?

283. If your significant other always asked for a bite of your food would this bother

you?

8

BENEFIT OF THE COVENANT

(Questions on Sex)

"Keep the fire lit in your marriage and your life will be filled with warmth."

— Fawn Weaver

284. What was the attitude toward sex in your family? Was it talked about? Who taught you about sex?

285. What are you beliefs about abstaining from sex until marriage?

286. How can we express intimacy without having sex?

287. Is sexual fidelity an absolute necessity to have a good marriage?

288. How often do you need or expect sex in marriage?

289. How will we handle situations when our sex drives are not aligned?

290. Do you feel comfortable initiating sex?

291. Is there anything specific that you need to get in the mood for sex?

292. What turns you off sexually?

293. Can we comfortably and openly discuss our sexual needs, preferences and fears?

294. If I desired more or less sex how should I approach you about it?

295. If our sex life is no longer meeting my needs, how can I bring this to your attention without offending you?

296. How do you relieve sexual frustration?

297. What are your views about masturbation and pornography?

298. Do you have any medical conditions that prevent you from having sex?

299. Do you use sex to self-medicate or as an emotional outlet?

300. Have you struggled with your sexual identity?

301. Have you ever had relations with someone of the same sex?

9

THE NEXT GENERATION

(Questions about Children)

"Children are gifts from the Lord.
They are fruits of His labor, through
acts of love in the bond of marriage"

-Elijah Mcleon

302. Do you currently have children? If not, do you want children?

303. How many children do you want?

304. Is it critical that we have children?

305. How soon do you expect to have children?

306. In the event one of us cannot have children, would that change the tone of our relationship?

307. Are you willing to try other ways of having children? i.e. - Adoption?

308. What makes a good parent?

309. What are your views on discipline?

310. Who will be the disciplinarian?

311. How do you plan on training up our children?

312. What values do you want to instill in our children?

313. What diet would you want to raise our children on?

314. What type of

schooling do you prefer our

children to have?

315. How will we invest in

our children's education?

316. How will we promote

spiritual and mental maturity in

our children?

317. Is it important for our

children to have God parents?

318.

If one of our children entertained a lifestyle we did not agree with, would you still be loving and supportive?

10

KEEPING THE PEACE

(Questions on Blended Families)

"A step parent is so much more than just a parent; they made the choice to love when they didn't have to."

-Nichole Valentin

319. What is your relationship like with the mother/father of your child?

320. What is your relationship like with your children?

321. Do you think it is okay to communicate with the mother/father of your child for reasons outside of your child?

322. What are your

expectations for a step parent?

323. How do you feel

about your significant other

disciplining your child?

324. Do you think it is

necessary to inform your child's

parent before you propose?

325. Is it appropriate for

the father/mother of your child

to meet your significant other?

If so when?

326. When is an

appropriate time to introduce

your children to your significant

other?

327. How would you feel

if my child/and or children lived

with us full-time?

11

LET YOUR IMAGINATION RUN WILD

(Situational Questions)

"Color outside the lines, let yourself daydream, agree with your imagination and laugh at the rules."

-Unknown

328. If one of us were to be

offered a career opportunity in a

location far from family, would

you be willing to move? If not,

would you be okay with having

a long distance relationship?

329. If we were offered

$50,000 an episode to be on a

reality show that doesn't reflect

our values and beliefs, would

you be interested?

330. If our teenage child

came to us and informed us that

they were pregnant, would you

recommend abortion or

adoption rather than raising the

child?

331. If you knew that in

one year you would die

suddenly, would you change

anything about the way you are

living now? If so, what would

you change?

332. If my ex and I had a

successful business together that

we continued to operate after

the relationship ended, would

you have an issue with them as

my business partner?

333. If I were to get my

tubes tied or a vasectomy and

didn't inform you would you

feel betrayed?

334. If you were to leave

money laying around and I took

it would you consider that

stealing?

335. Would you eat

crickets for $1,000?

336. Would you jump out

of an airplane for $5,000?

337. If you had $40,000

would you have sex

reassignment surgery?

338. Tell me a joke.

339. If you were having

lunch with five people you

respect and admire. They all

start criticizing a close friend of

yours, not knowing she is your

friend. What do you do?

12

FINAL THOUGHTS

(Questions to Ask Yourself)

"Our life is the sum total of all the decisions we make every day, and those decisions are determined by our priorities."

-Myles Munroe

340. Do I see myself

sharing the rest of my life with

this person?

341. If nothing about my

partner changed, could I live

with who and how they are for

the rest of my life?

342. Am I at peace moving

forward in this relationship?

Made in the USA
Monee, IL
27 February 2020